Let's visit
BOLIVIA

JOHN GRIFFITHS

SUMMITVLLE 948.052

Griffiths

ACKNOWLEDGEMENTS

The Author and Publishers are grateful to the following organizations and individuals for permission to reproduce copyright photographs in this book:

Andes Press Agency and Julio Etchart; Steve Benson Slide Bureau; David Hudson; Eugénie Peter; Travel Photo International and Photothèque Vautier-de Nanxe.

The author also wishes to thank Señor Gonzalo Alborta of the Bolivian Embassy in London and Ms. Lucy Chamberlain who typed his text from a difficult original manuscript.

CIP data
Griffiths, John
   Let's visit Bolivia
   1. Bolivia – Social life and customs – Juvenile literature
   I. Title
   948'.052   F3308

   ISBN 0 222 00946 2

Burke Publishing Company Limited
Pegasus House, 116-120 Golden Lane, London EC1Y 0TL, England.
Burke Publishing (Canada) Limited
Registered Office: 20 Queen Street West, Suite 3000, Box 30, Toronto, Canada M5H 1V5.
Burke Publishing Company Inc.
Registered Office: 333 State Street, PO Box 1740, Bridgeport, Connecticut 06601, U.S.A.
Filmset in Baskerville by Graphiti (Hull) Ltd., Hull, England.
Printed in Singapore by Tien Wah Press (Pte.) Ltd.

Contents

"A Little Marvel"

This Bolivian republic has a particular charm for me. First its name, then all the advantages; with not one drawback, it seems it was ordered to be hand-made! The more I think about the good fortune of this country, the more it appears to me a little marvel.

Perhaps Simon Bolivar described Bolivia in such glowing terms in 1825 because his own name had been taken for this newly-independent country. The honour was not unjustified: this Venezuelan general had liberated much of South America from the Spaniards at the beginning of the nineteenth century. However, Bolivia, previously known as Upper Peru (Alto Peru), was to experience many disasters before beginning to enjoy the "good fortune" of which Bolivar spoke.

Nor is modern Bolivia a "little country". It consists of 1,098,580 square kilometres (424,160 square miles)—more than the whole of France, Spain and Portugal combined but less than half the original area of the country at the time of independence from Spain. Bolivia's territory has been nibbled away by all her neighbours—Argentina, Chile, Peru, Paraguay and Brazil. Wars have cost the country her outlet to the Pacific Ocean as well as part of her territory. Even so, Bolivia is the fifth largest country in Latin America—after Brazil, Argentina, Peru and Colombia.

Inside this huge country every extreme of geography and climate may be found. Not for nothing has Bolivia been described as a "microcosm of the universe" (a world in miniature): its features include snow-covered peaks, fertile valleys, dense forests and tropical plains, sometimes only a car journey apart. The climate ranges from extremes of cold in the snows and biting air of the mountains in the west, through the more temperate climes of the valleys in the centre of the country, to the sweaty jungles and tropical plains in the north and east. Bolivia is one of the most beautiful of all Latin American countries but its beauty is combined with a harsh and varied climate and geography.

It is the Andean mountains, running down the entire length of the country like a bony spine, which give Bolivia such a variety of climates and which divide the country into the highlands, the Altiplano (high plateau), the valleys to the east of the mountains, the *yungas* (semi-tropical mountain valleys) and the Oriente (eastern lowlands).

The highlands contain the best known geographical feature of Bolivia—the huge mountain ranges which seem to act as a

A statue of Simon Bolivar (left) and José de San Martin, two of the most important figures in the struggle to free South American countries from Spanish rule

frame for the rest of the country. The west is dominated by two chains of the Andean mountains. The more westerly, known as the Cordillera Occidental (the Western Cordillera), stands majestically between Bolivia and Chile, and the Pacific coast. The whole range averages 5,030 metres (16,500 feet) above sea level, and rises to 6,530 metres (21,420 feet) in the peaks of the Sajama. The eastern chain of mountains is known as the Cordillera Real (the Royal Cordillera). It runs south-

9

A view of the River Pilcomayo, in the Cordillera Occidental

east, completely encircling Lake Titicaca—one of the highest
lakes in the world at 3,810 metres (12,500 feet) above sea
level—then due south through the centre of Bolivia.

Between these two mountain ranges is the Altiplano, a high
plateau on which about seventy per cent of Bolivia's population lives. The climate of this Altiplano region is generally cool
throughout the year; even during the warmer rainy season from
November until March the nights are always cold. The rainy
season is the time for agricultural growth in the area but few
crops survive the cold, the low rainfall, and the effects of the
poor soil. For this reason, livestock is important—in particular

10

llamas, alpacas, and sheep. At the northern end of the Altiplano, near Lake Titicaca, more crops are grown since the climate is less harsh. Half of Lake Titicaca is in Peru. The lake provides a vital link between that country and Bolivia, and a means of access for Bolivia, through Peru, to the Pacific coast.

The Altiplano—and especially La Paz, the best-known city in the region—is notorious for *sorojche,* a "mountain-sickness" caused by the altitude and lack of oxygen. La Paz is at an altitude of 3,650 metres (12,000 feet). The whole of the Altiplano is between 3,650 and 4,000 metres (12,000 and 13,000 feet) above sea level and is thus one of the highest regions in the

Campesino shepherds and their flock, on the Bolivian Altiplano. Few crops survive in this climate, and therefore livestock is particularly important

Aymara Indians working in the thin soil of the Altiplano. Too poor to buy an ox to pull the ploughshare, these people are tilling the ground in much the same way as their ancestors did centuries ago

world. Some travellers to Bolivia find *sorojche* unbearable and soon leave—most acclimatize to the altitude after resting and drinking a tea made from *coca* leaves. Even then they may find that any physical exertion in this region of Bolivia seems more than usually difficult. However, the native American Indian people—the Aymaras and Quechuas—appear to be completely used to living at the high altitudes of the highlands and the Altiplano.

The eastern slopes of the mountains fall away gradually towards the eastern plains in a jumble of hills and gorges, joined by fertile valleys. These are the semi-tropical mountain

12

valleys of the Cordillera Real, called the *yungas* (which is an Aymara word). Water, in short supply on the Altiplano, is found here in abundance. Rain feeds a multitude of streams and the lushness of the vegetation more than makes up for the dryness and desolation of the highlands and Altiplano region. Rich forests line the slopes, while the valleys are thick with a great variety of plant-life. It is here that *coca* is grown. This plant is important in the day-to-day lives of the Bolivian people, not

The *yungas,* or semi-tropical mountain valleys of the Cordillera Real – a sharp contrast to the arid, infertile soil of the Altiplano

least because it is a source of the drug cocaine. As such, it provides much of the income of the region. Here, too, sometimes completely isolated from the outside world, are to be found settlements of Bolivian Indians, whose families have lived in the area from pre-Colombian times: that is, from before the Spanish Conquest.

The largest valley regions of Bolivia are at Cochabamba, Sucre and Tarija. They are the source of most of the country's agricultural produce—wheat, maize, barley, grapes and groundnuts. Cochabamba has long been known as "the granary of Bolivia", while, in Chuquisaca and Tarija tobacco and fruits such as apricots and peaches are grown. In recent years much

A fertile valley in Cochabamba, the "granary of Bolivia"

A farm in Tarija province, built in Spanish colonial style. Much of Bolivia's agricultural produce comes from this area

progress has been made in these mainly agricultural areas of Bolivia.

The region of the eastern lowlands, know as the Oriente, represents about seventy per cent of all Bolivian territory. It is made up of the tropical forests of the Amazon basin, enormous areas of natural pasture, and open forests in the south. In most of this region rainfall is high, although in some areas flooding is followed each year by drought. The climate is generally hot, though cold winds do occasionally blow from the south, bringing sand- and dust-storms, called *surazos*. Consider-

15

ing its size and rich natural resources, the Oriente has been a neglected part of Bolivia. Transport is poor—largely by a river system, as there are few roads. Transport and communication difficulties have tended to isolate this area from the rest of Bolivia, and from the rest of the world, and have held back its development.

Due to its size, the Oriente is divided into a number of sub-regions. The Upper Beni begins at the northern border of Bolivia and runs south to include the department of Pando and about half the department of El Beni. (Bolivia is divided into departments which correspond to counties or states in other countries.) This is the sub-region covered in tropical rain forests where the *hevea* (rubber tree) grows. In the past, the crude rubber was collected by travelling people called *siringas,* transferred in canoes, or dug-outs made from a single log, to collection points and from these to the rest of the world. Few people have settled in the Upper Beni. Many are deterred by the unhealthily damp climate, the tropical diseases and the parasitic insects.

The sub-region of Santa Cruz consists of the southern end of El Beni and the northern two-thirds of the department of Santa Cruz. Unlike the Upper Beni, this semi-tropical area is relatively healthy and free of diseases and parasites. As a result, it has been able to develop its considerable natural resources. A wide variety of crops is grown; and the discovery of oil and natural gas has caused an increase in prosperity and led to a huge growth in population.

16

The Chaco, the southernmost sub-region of the Oriente, is probably the least hospitable part of Bolivia. For seven or eight months of the year it suffers from drought, while during the remaining rainy season it is like a swamp. There is little agriculture in this area. The few people who live here raise cattle, sometimes selling large herds in neighbouring Paraguay or Argentina.

Tiahuanaco—Cradle of American Civilization

The Indian people of Bolivia, the Aymaras and Quechuas, know nothing of their ancestors. The early history of Bolivia is shrouded in mystery. Yet the country was the centre of Andean civilization—the civilization which led to the great empire of the Incas.

There was no written history of what came to be known as Bolivia until the arrival of the *Conquistadores* from Spain in the sixteenth century. The Spaniards not only wrote about what they saw: they also learned as much as they could about what had gone on before the time of the Incas. Unfortunately, they were able to learn very little because the Incas had tried to destroy all traces of the people before them so that they themselves appeared more important. Archaeological exploration has shown, however, that there were important earlier cultures.

The most important of the pre-Inca cultures was to be found at Tiahuanaco near to Lake Titicaca on the Bolivian-Peruvian

A huge monolith at Tiahuanaco, the centre of the most important pre-Inca culture in the Andes. This statue is four metres (over thirteen feet) high

border. This was undoubtedly the centre of a powerful people whose influence stretched as far as Colombia in the north, Peru in the west, and Chile and Argentina in the south. At Tiahuanaco are to be found the extensive ruins of stone constructions, carved out of solid rock by a people who had neither iron to make tools nor wheeled vehicles for transporting materials. What remains of this impressive monument are the huge stairways and terraces which formed the pyramidal shape of the structure. People from all over the world come to gaze

19

A huge stairway at Tiahuanaco, carved out of solid rock hundreds of years ago by people who had only the most basic tools

at the ornate carvings of the faces of the sun and moon—the most perfect examples of what remains at Tiahuanaco.

Yet we know almost nothing about the people who made Tiahuanaco. The sheer effort involved in quarrying the stone and moving it 4,000 metres (13,000 feet) up the Altiplano is amazing. The construction work is similarly impressive and must have been carried out over several generations. But what was Tiahuanaco? Was it a religious culture? A market, like many of the villages around Tiahuanaco today? Or was it the centre of a great empire preceding that of the Incas? It could have been each or all three of these things—we simply do not know. Nor, for that matter, do we know why Tiahuanaco fell in the ninth century.

Tiahuanaco could well have been the birthplace of American culture. Certainly, it has had an influence on much of Latin America. In Bolivia itself, the area of Lake Titicaca, near to Tiahuanaco, is a very important source of myths and legends.

When the Spaniards arrived in what came to be known as Bolivia, they asked when Tiahuanaco was built. The local Indian people just laughed. All they knew from their forefathers, they said, was that the buildings had arrived overnight. The Incas almost certainly built upon the empire of the people at Tiahuanaco. They also took over the symbols of the sun gods

The Sun Gate at Tiahuanaco, showing a representation of the Inca Sun God and calendar

who wept tears in the shape of a snake's head and in the shape of a condor's head. They took over, too, the totem figures of the condor (a large South American vulture), the puma and the llama which are still found on the pottery of the region. In legend, the condor, with its enormous wingspan, was the messenger of the sun and able to fly to the gods.

Around A.D. 1200, with the growth of the Inca empire, the centre of power was moved from Bolivia to Peru, to the fertile valley of Cuzco in the Peruvian Sierra. The scale of organization and the magnificent wealth of the Inca empire were spectacular.

The Incas were said to have had supernatural origins at Lake Titicaca. On the island of Titicaca (meaning "jaguar rock"—the jaguar being the symbol of the Incas), the Sun God gave his descendents, Manco Capac and Mama Ojilo, the task of spreading civilization among the ignorant and barbarian races. According to legend, they were told to travel until the gold staff held by Manco Capac sank into the ground of its own accord. This happened at Cuzco where the royal pair set up the centre of their new empire. By the time the Spaniards arrived in South America, the land controlled by the Incas stretched over more than 984,000 square kilometres (380,000 square miles). Their empire covered the major part of the western half of the Latin American continent. Nor was it a collection of isolated parts: criss-cross roads connected one end to the other and relay runners, called *chasquis,* delivered messages probably more quickly than modern letters are delivered today.

22

A view of the island of Titicaca, taken from the Bolivian mainland

By the mid-fourteenth century, the highlands of Bolivia had become part of the "Four Quarters of the World"—as the Inca empire was called—along with part of the province of Kollasuya which included the Lake Titicaca area, what is now Peru, and the northern parts of Chile and Argentina. Today, the people of La Paz are still called Kollas (after Kollasuya). The rise of the Incas saw the rise of the Quechua Indian people over the Aymara Indian people. It may have been that the Incas were Quechuas but, whether or not this was so, the Quechuan language was made official throughout the Inca empire. The Quechuas who today live in the southern and eastern parts of the Bolivian Altiplano were probably settled there by the Incas.

23

Under the Inca agricultural system, which was very productive, a group of Indian families (called an *ayllu*), would farm their own land communally as well as work on land belonging to the Incas. Indians occupied the lowest place in the Inca society but could expect to be supported in times of hardship. This support, as well as the Inca wealth and power, ceased to exist when the Spaniards conquered the Americas.

Francisco Pizzaro landed in Peru in 1532. He captured the Inca leader Atahualpa, and ransomed him for gold—enough to fill an entire room to the height of a man's outstretched hand. The ransom was brought to Cajamarca, where Atahualpa was held, on the backs of column after column of llamas, weighed down with gold from the Four Quarters of the World. However, not even this could save Atahualpa. When he was put to death most cruelly by the Spaniards, the end of Inca rule was complete.

The Spaniards were quick to extend their control over the region. Silver mines were established and the immense wealth of the town of Potosi (discovered in 1545) attracted settlers like bees to the honey-pot. Chuquisaca—still at that time the official capital of Bolivia—had already been founded. Its site offered a warm sheltered valley, more than adequate water and fertile soil. La Paz, the modern capital, took its place because it was on the silver route to the coast and soon developed into a thriving, bustling town, although unable to rival the wealth of Potosi or the culture of Chuquisaca. By the end of the sixteenth century, Cochabamba and Tarija had also been founded, thus establishing the beginnings of the most important cities and towns in modern Bolivia.

The Spaniards seemed interested only in two things: religion, and the incredible mineral wealth of Bolivia. It was the Indian people who suffered as a result. They were cruelly used in the silver mines as virtual slaves, under a system known as *mita*. Though a minority of Spanish priests and missionaries tried to improve conditions for the Indians, between ninety and ninety-five per cent of them had disappeared within a century of Spanish occupation. They died from the combined effects of harsh treatment and foreign diseases. However, not all Indians remained docile in the face of such adversity and, in 1781, the Indian leader Tupac Amaru led a long and well-supported uprising against Spanish rule. This preceded the general uprising against the Spaniards which was about to erupt throughout Latin America.

For, as Bolivia and the other Latin American countries became more wealthy and settled, the Spanish presence became harder to bear. People born in Latin America—*Criollos*—could not tolerate the governing of their countries by Spanish people—*Peninsulares*—and Spanish laws. One country after another demanded its independence. Chuquisaca in Bolivia was the site of the first rebellion in Latin America against Spain, though Bolivia was the last country, in 1825, to gain its freedom.

But freedom from Spain brought neither peace nor security nor prosperity. The most capable leader of Bolivia after its

A Quechua Indian — his hat is reminiscent of the helmets worn by the Spanish conquistadors

independence, Santa Cruz, remained President for ten years. But, after his defeat in 1839, Bolivia suffered more than thirty years of civil strife under a series of brutal dictators. During this time the country's relations with its neighbours became worse, leading (in 1860) to a treaty with Brazil under the terms of which Bolivia gave away 1,000 square kilometres (386 square miles) of land in the Amazon basin. A further disaster was the War of the Pacific fought from 1879-1883, in which Bolivia lost to Chile all her land along the Pacific coast as well as the valuable nitrate deposits in the region. Later, in the Chaco War of the 1930s, she was to become completely land-locked, losing access to the Pacific Ocean through the River Paraguay.

After the War of the Pacific, Bolivia enjoyed a period of calm and peace during which time the "tin barons" emerged. The Patiño, Aramayo, Hochschild and Suarez families all became tremendously rich from Bolivian mineral resources—particularly from tin, as demand for this mineral increased with the growth of food-canning industries. From the 1920s, however, the outward calm of Bolivia hid internal unrest. The Chaco War of the 1930s against Paraguay, and an alarmingly rapid succession of presidents, destroyed Bolivia's image as a stable, peaceful Latin American country. The Bolivian revolution which began in La Paz in April 1952 only made things worse.

The Bolivian Revolution of 1952 and After

The Chaco War was one of many disasters for Bolivia. Gran Chaco is a plain. It is hot, dry and dusty in the west, and flooded in the east. Because of rumours of vast oil deposits there, war broke out between Bolivia and Paraguay. Over 100,000 soldiers were killed in the war, most of them Bolivian Indians forced to fight on unfamiliar ground for a cause they did not understand. Defeat was to bring into question many aspects of Bolivian life and politics and contribute to the revolution of 1952. Bolivia had other problems, too. Tin, the most important industry in Bolivia, had gone into decline after the 1920s. So, too, had agriculture. And now inflation added to the country's difficulties.

The revolution of 1952 began simply as another *coup,* a change of leaders. But Bolivian life was to be fundamentally affected. The MNR—the National Revolutionary Movement —was the main political party to come to power. It was led by Victor Paz Estensorro, and it quickly received the support

Victor Paz Estensorro, founder of the MNR and president of Bolivia from 1952 to 1964

of trade unions in the tin-mines who wanted better wages and working conditions. Ownership of the mines was taken away from the "tin barons". In the countryside, especially close to La Paz, there were demands for a better deal for country people. This fitted in with the new government's ideas of bringing the country people more into line with modern living. One way to do this was to return to the Indian people the land which had been taken away from them by the Spaniards. But the advanced agricultural system of the Incas

29

had fallen victim to the Spanish Conquest and the neglect of irrigation and terracing meant that farming was, at this stage, both backward and primitive. In the more remote areas of Bolivia it was, and remains, difficult to get country people to change their ways of doing things. However, in the Altiplano region, in the *yungas,* and in the fertile Cochabamba valley, there was enthusiasm for the Agrarian Reform of 1953 which gave back the land. At this time, the Indian people were also given a greater dignity by being referred to as *campesinos*— country people—rather than by the more dismissive term *Indio*—meaning simply, ''Indian''.

The immediate effects of the Agrarian Reform were not good. Food production decreased and, although it did subsequently rise again, by 1958 food constituted more than half of all Bolivia's imports. With a fall in tin prices, with wage increases, and with the need to import most of its food, the government was forced to turn to the United States for aid. This was the only way to save Bolivia from disaster, including probable starvation, but it slowed down some of the changes that had been planned. The revolution was unfinished.

By the 1960s Paz Estensorro was unable to hold his government and the country together. He was replaced, in a bloodless coup in 1964, by an army general named Rene Barrientos. The military were to play a very important and visible part in Bolivian political life from this time on, ruling the country in a strong and, some would say, harsh manner.

General Barrientos died in a helicopter crash in 1969.

Rene Barrientos, the army general who seized power from Paz Estensorro in 1964

During his period in power, Bolivia was the scene of a drama involving the Argentine revolutionary Ernesto ("Che") Guevara. Che had gone to Bolivia from Cuba (where he had been deeply involved in the revolution begun in 1959 to organize a revolution intended to spread to all the other countries of Latin America. He failed in his attempt, and this failure was to lead to his own death. Che was unable to make contact with the tin-miners who might have been sympathetic to his plans; he was also unable to communicate with the Indian people in whose

31

area he had set up a base, since he could not speak their language.

Once it was discovered that Che Guevara was in Bolivia, every effort was made to ensure his capture. After only six months' activity, in October 1967, he was seized and killed. His impact on Bolivia was only slight but for many people throughout the world, especially the young, Che had become a hero.

After Barrientos's death, the presidency soon returned to the military, with General Ovando and General Torres rising and falling in quick succession. The most stable presidency was that of General Hugo Banzer from 1971 to 1978. The seven years of Banzer's presidency saw an improvement in the Bolivian economy. Agriculture in the Santa Cruz area boomed with the growth of the sugar, cotton and coffee plantations. Brazil gave Bolivia ten million US dollars to build a new railway between Santa Cruz and Corumba on the Brazilian border. In return, Bolivia provided Brazil with natural gas, oil, rubber, iron and manganese. But the rise in the cost of living during this period caused real hardship to the country people and many of them blocked roads into Cochabamba in protest. President Banzer dealt very harshly with the striking peasants and, during 1977 and 1978, he lost much of his support—mainly because of the rising cost of living and the many hardships suffered by the people.

June 1978 was the date set for free elections in Bolivia but President Banzer was unwilling to give up power. The election was so obviously a fraud that even those close to the President were forced to admit this. When he spoke of handing power over to a military group, sections within the air force organized a coup and threatened to bomb La Paz. From that time on, Bolivia has seen a number of presidents in and out of the Palacio Quemado—the Presidential Palace—in speedy succession. Some have been strong, others weak; some from the military, others from civilian life. One was a woman. Bolivia has clearly suffered from this constant change of president and from the political instability.

The military coup of July 1980, the harshest of any in Bolivia's history, did much to darken the country's image abroad. Groups or individuals who challenged the authority of the group in power—the *junta* or ruling council—were very

The main government building in La Paz

President Banzer
addressing a rally in
La Paz. His presidency
saw a steady
improvement in the
Bolivian economy

severely treated: trade unionists, miners and members of the church all suffered. The junta were criticized from outside Bolivia for their alleged involvement in cocaine trafficking. Foremost amongst the critics was the United States government which was especially concerned about the danger of drugs. All US aid was cut off, along with aid from the EEC (European Economic Community). Food aid to Bolivia was only resumed in 1982 after assurances that the country would move towards civilian rule and that the cultivation of *coca,* from which cocaine is extracted, would be wiped out.

President Hernan Siles Zuazo took office in October 1982 with the first civilian government since 1978. He had been narrowly elected president in 1979 but was unable to take up his position. Now his government was greatly welcomed, not only inside Bolivia, but also by countries like the USA. He began his presidency severely handicapped: Congress, headed by many of his old political enemies, was largely unfriendly, while the economy was virtually in ruins. His allotted time in office was beset by problems, for there were many difficulties facing his country.

In July 1984 the President was ''kidnapped'' and held—for just twelve hours. It is still not clear whether this was a real kidnapping, or whether (as has been suggested) it was simply an attempt by the President to get rid of some of his opponents and win the sympathy of the people.

The People

The population of Bolivia which numbers 6,000,500, is mainly Indian, and society is divided into Indians, whites and Cholos—a mixture of the other two races.

The Indians come from three different groups: the Quechuas, the Aymaras and the Guaranis. All three have their own languages although Spanish is the main language of Bolivia. The Quechuas, the largest group (numbering over one million), live on the outer rim of the Altiplano and in the valleys. Quechuas are considered to be more cheerful than the Aymaras, the second most important group, who live in the northern Altiplano, on the mountain slopes and in the *yungas*. The Aymaras are a conservative people, much less outgoing than the Quechuas. The Guarani population is small and lives near the border with Paraguay.

At the time of Spanish colonization, another Indian tribe, called the Urus, lived around Lake Poopo, south of Oruro. (Uru-Uru means many Uru). There were also groups of Urus

Uru reed boats on Lake Titicaca

living on floating rafts made of *totora* reed on Lake Titicaca, eating roots and raw fish they caught from the lake. This tribe more or less died out in the 1960s although small groups still exist. A number of Chipaya Indians live in the south of the Altiplano, still using the style of dress imposed upon them by Spanish missionaries in the sixteenth century.

The Aymaras and Quechuas have a mongoloid appearance like that of the Eskimoes. This raises further questions about the history and origin of the Bolivian Indians. Where did they come from? Did they cross into the Behring Straits from Asia, making their way to South America at the end of the Ice Age? We shall never know, but even if they were immigrant peoples, the Quechuas and Aymaras are now firmly settled in Bolivia.

Both the Quechuas and Aymaras are capable of great feats of endurance. They can work for long periods in the most miserable of conditions, suffering cold, heat, hunger and even pain—though it is likely that only the constant chewing of *coca* leaves makes any of this possible.

Under the Incas, *coca*-chewing was restricted to the leaders of the people but within a few years of the arrival of the Spaniards the habit had become widespread. The chewing of *coca* is addictive, but in modern Bolivia every Indian person from a very early age regards it as a necessity of life—like coffee-drinking in the USA or tea-drinking in Britain. Its

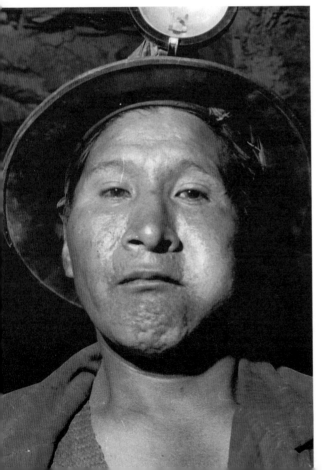

A tin-miner, his cheek puffed out with a wad of *coca* which he is chewing to numb his pangs of hunger, pain and fatigue

effects are to dull the senses and especially to ward off hunger, pain, cold and fatigue. Miners working in extreme cold, or up to their waists in water, could simply not survive without *coca*. Understandably, attempts to wipe out *coca*-growing in the *yungas*, where it is known as "green gold", have met with fierce resistance. These attempts are in response to the concern of foreign governments over the growth of trafficking in cocaine. In an attempt to deal with a social problem at home, however, the United States government has threatened the daily routine of Bolivian Indians whose life and culture revolve around *coca*.

Bolivian Indians, as descendants of the Incas who made the Andes a habitable place for man, believe themselves to be the true heirs to the land. They regard white people, like the Spaniards of the past who took away their land, with great suspicion and resentment. Most Indians live on plots that have been owned by the family for generations and they are fiercely defensive of their heritage. Even though they may be aware that theirs is not the best or most fertile land, they are generally suspicious of attempts to settle them elsewhere. The lure of towns and cities is not strong for these people: they know that, lacking education, the only kind of work they would find would be as "beasts of burden", carrying huge loads on their backs. On the land the *campesino* may work hard, and for long hours, but he is part of the life there, like his ancestors before him. These people are linked to the soil by centuries of occupation.

Campesinos ploughing their land with an ox-drawn wooden plough

The Cholos—the group of mixed white and Indian peoples— are growing in numbers and hold a middle position in society. Some own and work the land but the majority are employed in a variety of other occupations. A successful Cholo, educated and able to educate his children, may rise in Bolivian society.

The whites are a minority group in Bolivia, but it is they who rule the country—in their own interests.

The Cochabambinos—the people of Cochabamba—are regarded as the go-getters of Bolivia. It is they who are the businessmen and the politicians. Simon Patiño, one of the most famous of the "tin barons", came from Cochabamba, and he set an example for others to follow.

40

The Tarijeno—from Tarija—is the complete opposite of the Cochabambino, and the butt of many a joke. Like the stereotype Latin American, he is pictured as slow and lazy and, in his case, lounging on the bank of the River Guadalquivir. This joke is as unfunny to the Tarijeno in Bolivia as it is to the Pole in the USA or the Irishman in Britain. Another stereotype, the Chuquisaqueño—from Sucre in Chuquisaca—is regarded as a very conservative person, who behaves as if he were still living in the nineteenth century.

Lacking education, the only work these Indians have been able to find in the town is as "beasts of burden", carrying huge loads on their backs

Cochabamba *campesinas,* wearing beautiful, tall white hats. The number of black ribbons on a hat denotes whether the wearer is single, married or widowed

Whereas it is always likely but never certain that the succesful businessman or politician comes from Cochabamba, the origins of others are much more obvious. Bolivian *campesinas*—country women—give themselves away by their hats. Those of the Cochabamba *campesinas* are tall, white and wide-brimmed, and have black ribbons to indicate whether their wearers are single, married or widowed. The hats themselves are works of art; it takes one person a whole month to make the hand-crotcheted material which then has to be starched and shaped. A white oxide gives the hat its brightness. Women from all parts of Bolivia can be identified by their headgear. The women of La Paz, predominantly Aymaras, wear the black bowler usually associated with the Andean countries. The Quechua women in the south and east of the country wear a tall stove-pipe hat similar to the Welsh woman's traditional hat. In warmer areas, such as the Cochabamba valley, the hat is white with a black ribbon. In Oruro, part of the colder uplands, bowlers are also worn but always at a jaunty angle. In Potosi, a variety of hats are worn in dark brown, black or bottle green felt. At *fiesta* time hats become heavier as they are then decorated with sequins and pearls.

Bolivian women wear hats not only for protection but also as a symbol of wealth and position. A man's status can be assessed by the number of hats his wife owns. Little girls wear exact replicas of their mother's dress, even to the hat which may be a hand-me-down several sizes too large. However poor she is, a Bolivian woman will never appear bareheaded.

A Quechua Indian woman, wearing a traditional tall stove-pipe hat

Despite the 1952 revolution which did effect changes, especially for country people, the Bolivian standard of living is generally low. Most people live in miserably poor housing, and are inadequately fed and clothed. For many, education is non-existent and social services to help the old, the poor, the sick and the unemployed are confined mainly to the mines and to towns like La Paz.

There is, of course, a great difference in the standard of living

44

between town and country. People generally eat better in the towns where there are more wage-earners. But the diet of most Bolivians is deficient, lacking fats and proteins. Milk is enjoyed only by the minority. Fruit and vegetables are rare on the Altiplano due to transport problems and the inability of the *campesino* family to afford them. The diet in the highlands (generally agreed to be the home of the potato) consists of *chuño* (a dried form of potato), *quinoa* (a kind of millet) and a little maize. Bread is absent from the diet but, being unfamiliar, it is not missed.

Even in the east, around the wealthier Santa Cruz area, the diet is not much more varied, although meat, *yucca* (a root crop), bananas, coffee and sugar can all be obtained if the buyer can afford the price. Fruits are eaten when in season, but vegetables and dairy produce are virtually unknown. Yet this area could provide a varied diet for its population.

Hats decorated with sequins for fiesta time

A *campesino* family outside their home—even the children wear hats

Many Bolivians are still outside a money economy—that is to say, they barter or exchange those things they have for those things they need or want, rather than buying them for money. So peasant agricultural producers will eat most of what they produce and buy nothing in the markets, except perhaps some *coca* leaves to take away their hunger pangs.

Considering the poor diet and living conditions of most Bolivian people, it is not surprising that their health is similarly poor. Many still have to be convinced of the superiority of modern medicine over ancient remedies, the ingredients for

46

which are sold in all the street markets. The services of traditional witch doctors are very much in demand. A variety of diseases still exist throughout the country despite continuing programmes to wipe these out. However, the size of Bolivia and the dispersal of its population make it difficult to eradicate disease. Birth- and death-rates are high; life expectancy is generally low.

There are few schools in Bolivia and many people, particularly those who live in the countryside, cannot read or write. Bolivia's rate of illiteracy is one of the highest in Latin America. There are eight universities (La Paz, Cochabamba, Santa Cruz, Oruro, Potasi, Sucre, Trinidad and Tarija) but these are mostly attended by the well-off whose careers frequently have little to do with solving Bolivia's problems as a poor and backward country.

The Country

Bolivia is divided into the nine departments of La Paz (sixteen provinces), Cochabamba (fourteen provinces), Chuquisaca (nine provinces), Potosi (thirteen provinces), Oruro (six provinces), Santa Cruz (eleven provinces), Tarija (six provinces), the Beni (eight provinces) and Pando (four provinces). Additionally, there are three *delegaciones* which lie outside the system of departments. They are the national *delegacione* of Guarayos with its capital in Ascension, the *delegacione* of Chapare with its capital in Todos Santos and the *delegacione* of Gran Chaco with its capital in Villa Montes. Each is supervised by a *delegado* (delegate) appointed by the president.

Each department is in the charge of a prefect appointed by the president and responsible to him or her. The prefect has wide powers in his/her department and has authority over all local decisions although final authority rests with the president of the Republic.

Cantons, which are like villages or small towns, are controlled

48

by *corregidores* (magistrates), appointed by department prefects. Larger towns are presided over by an *alcalde*—or mayor. Very often Indian societies are organized in traditional *ayllus* (clans) controlled by *jilakatas* or *mallcus* (headmen or chiefs). These Indian organizations are not officially recognized but their moral authority is, nevertheless, very strong.

The most important city of Bolivia is La Paz which began as a stopping-off point on the way from Potosi to Lima in Peru. La Paz is at the foot of a deep canyon over which towers Mount Illimani's snow-covered peak. The neighbouring peaks of Illampu and Huayña Potosi protect the city from the winds of the Altiplano. They also help to produce the rain which falls daily from December through to February.

La Paz's position in the canyon has dictated the way it has developed. Unable to adopt the neat street plans of cities elsewhere in Latin America, it has taken on a "spoon" shape. The *adobe* houses of the Aymaras are set in the slope of the canyon. They are made from dried earth and they are sometimes washed away during the rainy season. The oldest buildings in La Paz are found on the slope, like the sixteenth-century Church of San Sebastian and the house of the Aymara Chief Quirquincha.

The streets of La Paz are steep, descending to the city centre, leaving the poorer houses of the Aymaras behind. The city centre is the rich area, with smart new hotels and office blocks. Beyond them is the "handle" of the "spoon", containing the lower, sunnier houses of the wealthy of La Paz.

49

However, all areas suffer from the same appalling lack of sanitation and limited water supply. La Paz—with its one million population— is growing, like all cities; by the year 2010 it may have between 1.5 and 2.5 million people. Only in the 1970s did the government begin to take an interest in La Paz's development. In the four hundred years up to that time it was allowed to grow without any regulation.

The same could be said of Santa Cruz, the second largest Bolivian city with some 400,000 inhabitants. For four hundred years it remained virtually unchanged. Only in the 1950s did it start to grow again as the economy, through agriculture and oil, began to prosper. The department of Santa Cruz

Mount Illimani's snow-covered peak, which towers above the city of La Paz

A general view of the city of La Paz

represents one-third of the country and is Bolivia's largest and richest department.

Cruzeños—the people of Santa Cruz—are famous for their independence and Santa Cruz city still resembles the cowboy-town it once was—hitching-rails may be found in the streets. Of all the regions of Bolivia, Santa Cruz has been the most prosperous—perhaps because it has always been separate from the rest of the country.

Santa Cruz began to develop and grow in the 1950s when a modern road reached it for the first time. It now also has railway links with Argentina and Brazil which provide markets

51

for its produce. At the time when the road was completed ,Gulf Oil discovered its first deposits south of Santa Cruz city. This was the making of Santa Cruz, for it derives its income from a tax on oil and gas. Bolivia's own oil company, along with a number of other companies, has also discovered oil to the north. Santa Cruz has developed its own refining industry and has an industrial area near by, making textiles, plastics and wood products.

The department of Santa Cruz is a farming region; cattle are raised here and local crops include sugar, cotton, rice and soya beans. In the north, rubber trees grow wild and the rubber

Sugar is one of the crops grown in the area around Santa Cruz. This picture shows refined sugar being put into sacks

has yet to be properly harvested. The region is so rich in hardwoods that even window frames and packing-cases are made out of mahogany. However, Santa Cruz has, like the rest of Bolivia, a transportation problem. The area is a long way from the coast and transport costs make all its products very expensive. Yet Santa Cruz has hardly begun to exploit its natural resources. Only a fraction of the available land is currently being used. The government has tried to attract *campesinos* down from the less fertile, inhospitable Altiplano but, so far, without success. Instead, immigrants have come from outside the region and from other countries. There are two large settlements of Mennonite farmers and several Japanese settlement areas. German settlers are long-established. And increasingly Chileans, Argentinians, Americans and Brazilians are moving in, for land here is probably as cheap as anywhere in the world.

In the late 1960s there were sloths in the trees and no lights in the streets, and the only transport was by jeep and ox-cart. When it rained boys would carry people across the muddy streets. Now that Santa Cruz has become the richest area of Bolivia things have changed.

Cochabamba is the Quechua equivalent of "water meadows", and this area has traditionally been Bolivia's larder, with seventy per cent of the population working in agriculture. Tiahuanacans migrated here to take advantage of the climate. They were later followed by the Incas and the Spaniards.

Cochabamba has three agricultural areas. First there is the

A vegetable stall in a Bolivian market

Altiplano region which produces over a quarter of Bolivia's potatoes and most of its lamb and mutton. Chapare is more tropical, producing exotic fruits like papayas and avocados, as well as timber and rice. Between the two is land which is ideal for dairy farming, raising poultry and growing cereals such as wheat, corn and maize, and a great variety of fruit and vegetables. A dam planned for this area will ensure its irrigation.

The Cochabaminos are famous for being ambitious go-getters. Simon Patiño, the "king of tin", is the fifth richest man in the world and the most famous Cochabambino of them

54

all. He began as a simple miner who, by luck, discovered a rich vein of tin and became astronomically wealthy. Yet he was never accepted by the landowners of Cochabamba who could not forget his humble origins. Made to feel an outsider, he left Bolivia for France in 1921 and divided his time between Paris and Biarritz. His home in Cochabamba had been the Palacio Portales, a vast palace that is a cross between a royal residence and a cathedral. In its grounds stands a huge boulder veined with the tin which was the source of his vast wealth.

Sucre is the capital of Bolivia. However, it is the capital in name only, for La Paz is the government nerve-centre of the country. The Supreme Court remains in Sucre which was the seat of Spanish colonial government in the region. Now, history

The Patiño family house in Cochabamba

has passed Sucre by and the city has become a quiet, beautiful reminder of what it once was. The descendents of the first Spanish settlers still live here, many of them in elegant Spanish colonial houses. Their ancestors made their fortunes in the silver-mines of Potosi, but chose to live in the better climate of Sucre. In colonial days Sucre was known as Chuquisaca, changing its name at the time of independence in honour of the French general responsible for chasing out the Spaniards.

In those colonial days, Sucre was a bustling, thriving city, known as the "Athens of America". The University of San Javier was set up here in the sixteenth century and its influence spread throughout the continent. Today the pace of life is much

The cloisters of *La Recoleta,* a church and monastery in Sucre—note the Spanish influence in the architecture

The balcony of a house in Sucre, built in Spanish style

slower. There is little or no industry—nor is there the prosperity associated with La Paz, Cochabamba and Santa Cruz. Sucre is a delightful city, peaceful and elegant. If it were anywhere else in the world it would attract hordes of tourists anxious to soak up its historic atmosphere. However, in Bolivia, tourism is a branch of the economy that has yet to be developed even though there is so much in the country to interest visitors.

The *pampas*—the wide natural prairies—of the Beni River in the south of Bolivia are the lands of the Mojos. The Mojos are a prosperous Indian group who live off the products of agriculture—fruits, yucca, sweet potatoes, tobacco, rice, sugarcane and cotton. Wild cattle have roamed this area for centuries. Now the Mojos, and farmers who have migrated to the area, raise more than half Bolivia's livestock; over 1.5 million— about ten per inhabitant of the country. The meat produced here goes to market in La Paz and elsewhere. Already more meat is produced here than can be consumed in Bolivia and export markets are very necessary. However, there is a problem with transportation, for this region is so cut off that everything must be flown in and out. The local farmers regard their single-engined planes much like cars and fly to wherever they want to go. Most of this area has no electricity, no telephone, no water supply or sanitation. And its people pay no taxes.

When this region was first settled, there were great natural hazards to contend with. Mosquitoes spread malaria and other diseases; the *jejenes*—a biting insect—would almost drive a person mad with irritation and the *borro* would lay its eggs in the skin, causing the sufferer great pain when it was necessary to cut out the hatched worm. As if these hazards were not unpleasant enough, the local rivers contained snakes, alligators and even piranha fish which can strip the flesh from an animal—or human—in minutes.

Things have changed. Prosperous farmers now generate their

The "Valley of the Moon" near La Paz—so called because erosion of the rock has given the area an appearance similar to that of the moon's surface

own electricity and communicate with the outside world with their own radio-transmitters. Some have their own swimming-pools. But virtually every item they need—including construction materials—has to be flown into the region. Like many other parts of Bolivia, the Beni has hardly been touched. The soil is good and could produce crops for consumers all over the world.

Religion and Superstition

Roman Catholicism is the main religion of Bolivia and the church plays an important part in Bolivian life. Yet Christianity has not completely replaced the pre-Colombian religions that existed before the Spanish conquest of the New World: rather it has been adapted to these earlier religions.

The Bolivian *campesino* is deeply superstitious. He regards mountain peaks, lakes and caves as the hiding-places of spirits which can either harm or reward him. Numerous myths reinforce his beliefs, many of which are based upon the history of Bolivia as well as on everyday life. For the Aymara, the world began with Verajocha who emerged from Lake Titicaca. Many myths concern the huge stone figures of Tiahuanaco. In one of them, Verajocha first created men of enormous size in a world without sun or warmth. Then, when they displeased him, he destroyed them in a flood, creating a new world with sun, moon and stars and a new race of mankind. Another myth is that Verajocha made the huge statues of Tiahuanaco himself as models of the new man. Verajocha's followers then went out into the world and made peoples and tribes from rocks, caverns and streams.

The *campesinos'* respect for things made of stone and the continuing regard for Inca symbols, such as the condor, are caught up in such legends. *Campesinos* also have a great respect for the mountains of the Andes. Each peak has its god—*achachila*—which is the ancestral spirit of the nearest valley or village. When Indians, like the Aymaras, are travelling and see an outward manifestation of an *achachila* for the first time, they kneel, take off their hats and offer the wad of *coca* leaves they have been chewing by throwing it on the ground or placing it on a rock. The *achachila* of the Urus was the mud of Lake Titicaca. But it is the mountains of Bolivia which dominate the landscape so it is hardly surprising that they should be so respected.

In 1898, an English explorer named Sir Martin Conway attempted to climb the highest mountain in Bolivia. This is the Illampu, the Inca Storm God. The local people, fearing the wrath of the mountain, first threatened Conway, then refused to act as his porters. Conway tried to climb the mountain by himself. He reached only half way.

At the other end of the Cordillera is a flat-topped mountain called the Mururata—Headless One. In Aymara mythology this is a "victim", a chieftain attacked by an Indian with a sling, knocking off his head with a fierce blow. According to the myth, the "head", or peak, fell to earth in the east, making the Sajama peak at the Chilean frontier. The blood of the chieftain

Mount Illampu, the highest mountain in Bolivia and the home of the Inca Storm God

fell to earth making the copper-mines of Corocoro. The Incas believed that even in the mines there were spirits—like the *Supay* who lived at the centre of the earth. The Indians regard the *Supay* as a spirit of evil which can give blessings and protection if suitably approached. Bolivian miners today placate a gentler spirit, Tio, who (they believe) lives in every mine. At each mine entrance there is a small clay or stone figure to whom they give their wad of *coca* as an offering. Miners are very superstitious and no priest or woman is welcome at a mine.

Pacha-Mama, the Earth Mother, has been worshipped since

62

Inca times. Even in the towns, people sprinkle a few drops of any drink on the ground—a custom called *ch'allar* which dates back to the Incas who poured offerings on the ground when they sowed their crops. But worship of Pacha-Mama is a country religion; in the rural areas one day a year is devoted to her, now usually during Easter. Small offerings are burned to Pacha-Mama and flowers and confetti are scattered about the house to bring good fortune to its occupants. At harvest time, or when new earth is broken, offerings are made; and when an animal is killed a few drops of blood are sprinkled on the ground to placate the spirits.

Mount Sajama on the Chilean frontier. According to Aymara mythology, this peak is the head of a chieftain who was killed by an Indian attacker

Ekeko is the god of good fortune from ancient times and still respected in modern Bolivia. January 24th is devoted each year to Ekeko; in La Paz this celebration is combined with celebrations for Our Lady of La Paz, the patron saint of the city. Ekeko is a round, jolly old man. Statues of him can be found in almost every Bolivian home. Many people carry models of him to bring good luck, for they believe that he has great powers. January 24th is also the time of the fair called *Alacitas*—which means "buy me". Legend has it that if something coveted is bought in miniature during the festival, then it will be owned in full size before the year is out. Miniature houses and animals are sold to many eager, sometimes desperate, buyers.

Fiestas—popular festivals and carnivals—are of great importance in Bolivia and are built around religious events. However, these are not really religious celebrations though the church is involved. Carnival, the fiesta just before Lent, is a major occasion. *Campesinos* travel to La Paz, Cochabamba, Oruro and Sucre where the largest carnivals are held; smaller ones may take place in villages. The Oruro Carnival is famous in Bolivia for its *diablada*—devil dancers—who are organized in the year preceding the carnival. It is a mixture of pagan and Christian elements as are all the carnivals. In addition to the carnival itself, there are markets, much dancing and much drinking.

In Oruro, the miners renew their allegiance to *La Virgen de Sucavon* (the Virgin of Sucavon Mine) who protects them when they are underground. In her honour they will dance as devils for days on end!

The "devils" are dressed in a breastplate beautifully embroidered with sequins and precious stones, a short skirt, divided into five leaves, and white tights. In his right hand each dancer holds a "viper"—or coloured scarf. But it is their masks that demand most attention. Each one has bulging eyes, horns, ears, tusks and a grinning mouth. Covered in jewels and brightly painted, the mask represents a three-headed viper or some other reptile.

Lucifer, or Satan, who follows the "devils" is even more extravagantly dressed. He wears a long cape, and has a flowing blond mane. And he wears an even larger mask. Behind him

Diablada (devil dancers) at the Oruro carnival. These dancers, in their colourful costumes, can be seen at carnivals throughout Bolivia

Dancers, in their colourful masks and costumes, at the Feast of the Virgin of Copacabana

comes the Archangel Michael. And, behind him, a brass band brings up the rear. Lucifer's wife—the China-Supay—completes the picture. This snake-like procession of dancers will continue dancing for four days before taking off their masks outside the Church of Oruro.

66

The other dance of the Oruro Carnival is the *morenada*. Here the dancers wear black masks and elaborately decorated skirts to represent the black slaves brought to the New World by the Spaniards. The Incas and Conquistadores are also represented. So too are the Tobas (a war-like tribe that once lived in the lowlands). They are dressed in headdresses and they carry spears.

Once the set-pieces of the carnival are over, it is the turn of the people to dance the *cueca*—a courtship dance brought from Spain, like the *flamenco* of Andalusia. The music is played on the *charanga*—an instrument made from the hollowed-out shell of a spiny armadillo—and on the guitar. Or they may dance the *huayños*, a dance from the Altiplano. The carnival always ends with the *kacharpaya,* the farewell dance of Bolivia.

Carnival is such an important time that workers and their families borrow money which it will take them a whole year to repay, just so that they can celebrate the occasion in style. There are stories in La Paz of people who selling their furniture, or their last animal, or even mortgaging their house so as to have enough money to celebrate the carnival in a suitable fashion.

The Catholic church in Bolivia has become less important since the 1952 revolution, but its position is still strong throughout the country, and particularly so in the towns and cities. The church has been criticized, however, for its lack of care for the needs of the country people of Bolivia whose education and standard of living are low. In the towns, the church does

**The cathedral
in La Paz**

provide schools but in the countryside the lack of education is all too sadly apparent.

Freedom of worship is guaranteed by law in Bolivia but there are few churches which are not of the Roman Catholic faith.

Minerals

All the minerals of modern Bolivia were known to the Incas although the mining of metals was but one part, a small part, of their lives. Before the Incas, copper was mined to make tools and decorations. Gold and silver were used mostly for decoration or in religious ceremonies. Later, bronze—an alloy of copper and tin—was made. This had a remarkable quality and hardness and was used for making tools and weapons.

The Incas regarded copper as a useful metal. Gold and silver they used for ornaments. The stone walls of the Inca palaces were often lined with gold. It was even used at times instead of cement! The clothes of the royal families were heavy with gold, silver and jewels. The *osno,* the royal chair upon which only an Inca could sit, was also made of gold. But these were really just decorations and when the Incas died their precious metals were buried with them. Lake Titicaca is reported to possess untold riches of gold, silver and jewels thrown into the lake by the Incas. However, no one has been able to find this treasure.

The Inca system of mining required Indians to work for two to three months a year in the mines. The Spaniards took over this system but offered the Indians none of the advantages offered by the Incas. The Indians became virtually slaves. The Spaniards were mainly interested in gold and silver and they ignored the other metals. Indians were tortured or bribed to show the Spaniards where the precious metals could be found. The first silver-mine was at Porco, near Potosi. For the Spaniards, however, the greatest discovery was Cerro Rico— the Rich Hill—found in 1545 by an Indian looking for a stray llama. It was one of the richest finds the world has ever known and from it, it has been calculated, a bridge of silver one metre (39.4 inches) wide could have been built from the New World to Spain. This bridge could have been matched by one made

A view of Potosi, with the Cerro Rico (Rich Hill) in the background. It was originally a silver mine, but now tin is mined there

from the bones of those who died digging the silver out of the earth. Potosi became well-known the world over. "As rich as Potosi", was the proverbial description of the greatest wealth anyone could aspire to.

By the end of the eighteenth century, the richest mines had been exhausted, and silver and gold became scarcer and more difficult to find. Bolivian minerals became important again at the end of the nineteenth century when the world was looking for metals for industry and, in particular, for the growing canning industries of Europe and North America. At Catavi, the Patiño family fortune was made with the discovery of a mountain seemingly made of tin. From that time tin has accounted for about eighty per cent of Bolivia's exports, with the Patiños providing half of that amount until the mines were nationalized in 1952 and passed into government ownership.

Simon Patiño may have become one of the richest men in the world but the miners who produce tin have stayed poor, working in terrible conditions. At Pulacayo, one of the most difficult mines in Bolivia, miners must work stripped to the waist, with water constantly sprinkled on their bodies to keep them cool. Yet the temperature outside the mine, high up in the Altiplano, is often below freezing. In Tipuani where gold is still mined, miners wearing only helmets and swimming trunks work up to their waist in water. This mine was worked by the Incas and the Spaniards, then by the Patiño family. Now it is run as a co-operative concern by the miners themselves. Tin-mining is dangerous and unhealthy. Most miners suffer

The dusty conditions in which miners have to work. Dust is a major health hazard and the average life expectancy of a Bolivian miner is only thirty-three years

from tuberculosis and silicosis, caused by the dust of the mines. Their life expectancy is just thirty-three years.

Bolivia, the world's second largest producer of tin, is also rich in other minerals. It is the largest producer of bismuth and a major supplier of metals such as antimony and tungsten. Silver, copper, lead, zinc and iron are all to be found in Bolivia as well as oil, phosphates and asbestos. The problem with Bolivian minerals has not been how to locate them but how to extract them easily and profitably. With Bolivia's transport difficulties and lack of resources, this has not been an easy matter. Recently, however considerable progress has been made in developing more of this great mineral wealth.

In the 1960s, plans were made to make Bolivia a producer of refined metals as well as a producer of ores. By the 1970s, the smelting of metal ores in Bolivia had begun, with plans for all ores to be treated within the country by the 1980s. Bolivia is now showing the world's experts just how wrong they were when they claimed that the high altitude of the Altiplano region would make it impossible for the country ever to smelt its own ores. Silver, so highly prized by the Spaniards, is still being produced in Bolivia, but almost as a by-product when lead and other metals are extracted.

Many metal industries are located in the area around Potosi. In the south-east, near the border with Paraguay, there are almost limitless supplies of iron ore and these are only now being developed due to the enormous transport problem. With Brazil and Argentina close by, and both requiring large quantities of

Miners returning from their work in the Cerro Rico tin-mines

iron and steel for their own development plans, Bolivia should have no problems finding buyers for its metals.

Bolivia is not a large producer of oil and gas but there are considerable deposits located in Santa Cruz, Chuquisaca and Tarija. And there are petroleum refineries at Cochabamba and Santa Cruz. Intensive exploration for oil and gas by Bolivian state-owned companies and by foreign oil companies (mostly from the US, but also from Spain, France and Canada) continues, with the hope of finding richer deposits. Bolivia is never likely to be in the ''big league'' of oil producers, but it should eventually be self-sufficient in oil, with a surplus left over for export.

Natural gas has grown in importance along with petroleum since the 1960s. From just one customer alone—neighbouring Argentina—Bolivia receives about one tenth of its export income. Brazil, too, is becoming important as a market for Bolivian natural gas with the possibility of a pipeline being built between the two countries. Argentina and Brazil provide the only markets for Bolivian natural gas until further new finds make it profitable to turn the gas into liquid and export it to more distant countries.

The history of Bolivia is intertwined with the history of mining—from the time of the civilization that preceded the Incas to the present day. The nineteenth century was marked by the fighting over the nitrate deposits on the Pacific coast which

The oil refinery in Cochabamba

led to the loss of Bolivia's outlet to the sea. The Chaco War was similarly about minerals—over the possibility of the existence of petroleum in the Gran Chaco region. And although the discovery and mining of tin made the tin barons wealthy, it provided few benefits for Bolivia.

Today, however, Bolivian miners have become a force to be reckoned with. They, like their counterparts in other parts of the world, have often been involved in political unrest because of the nature of their work and the harshness of their conditions. In 1941, many died along with their families in battles for better pay and conditions of work, in what has become

75

Workers from Catavi mine, demonstrating against appalling working conditions. Miners are a strong political force in Bolivia

known as the "Massacre of Catavi". In 1976, in the Siglo XX (Twentieth Century) mine, the miners went on strike by staying underground and were finally forced to work when soldiers moved into the mine with them. The 1952 revolution had already given the miners greater importance when the tin-mines were taken away from the "tin barons" and the miners assumed more responsibility for their running. Today, no political decision can be made in Bolivia without taking account of the miners, and of the Bolivian Workers Confederation (COB) to which all unions belong.

Transport

The train journey from Santa Cruz to Corumba on the Brazilian border is supposed to take twelve hours. The slowest time so far recorded is forty-three hours. This is just one example of the problem of transport in Bolivia.

Bolivia's particular problems of transportation are unique. These are caused by the mountain peaks of the Western Cordillera, the slopes which lead down through the valleys to the savannahs (grassy plains) in the east, and the equatorial rainforests on the Brazilian border. Most of the population (over seventy per cent) live on the Altiplano, whilst agriculture and mineral wealth are found long distances away locked in a difficult terrain. The problem is to bring the two together.

The Incas and the Spaniards used llama-trains for transportation; columns of the animals toiled up the Andes loaded with gold, silver or more mundane commodities. Even today llamas are used to carry blocks of salt from the salt-plains of Uyuni. It is said that llamas cry every morning until the sun rises for

Llama-trains such as this one were used by the Incas and the Spaniards centuries ago. Even today, the llama is an important means of transport in Bolivia

their Inca masters, the Sons of the Sun. The llama is an important part of the Bolivian economy: in addition to being a means of transport, it provides the Aymara with clothes and blankets from its wool, with fuel for warmth and cooking from its dung, with milk, and with meat.

Llama-trains were replaced by steam-trains with the coming of the railways at the end of the nineteenth century, although these did little more than connect the mines with the Pacific ports and with Argentina. The railway system in Bolivia is still inadequate despite recent investments in new equipment and lines. Railways have served only the interests of La Paz and the mining districts, with branches into the high valleys at Cochabamba and Sucre. Santa Cruz was without a railway until the 1950s when it was connected to neighbouring countries by branch lines. Bolivia has less than 3,220 kilometres (2,000 miles) of railway track, and large areas of the country have no rail communications due to their mountainous geography or to their lack (hitherto) of economic importance.

Rail travel in Bolivia used to be a risky business for travellers as far as dates and times were concerned, but recent improvements have increased its popularity. The "ferrobus" (bus/train) service to Cochabamba from La Paz now has to be booked a week in advance. However, rail travel is still slow—just 30 to 40 kilometres (18 to 24 miles) per hour—and will remain so until the tracks are improved. Weather and terrain also cause problems, with landslides in the mountain regions regularly blocking the lines.

In some areas roads have been preferred to railways but the roads are hardly better than the rail system. The mention of travelling by road was, until recently, enough to make a Bolivian groan in despair. Most roads were of poor quality. Until 1968, less than 965 kilometres (600 miles) were of asphalt or had gravelled surfaces out of a total of only 4,020 kilometres (2,500 miles). In the 1970s plans were begun to develop Bolivia's road system but there is still a long way to go, especially to improve road communications with the east of the country. The Pan

American Highway which enters Bolivia from Peru becomes little more than a dirt track by the time it leaves Bolivia and enters Argentina.

Great advances have been made in the system of building new roads and improving already existing ones. And there is now a long-term plan for this work. However, the deficiencies of road and rail transport have meant that Bolivia has leapt more or less from llama-trains to air transport, the latter being of enormous importance to the country.

Lloyd Aéro Boliviano, (LAB) the national airline, has an extensive network of international routes covering Latin America and the United States. But its internal services are of greater

A jungle road. Many Bolivian roads are little more than dirt-tracks, and this is a major factor in the country's transport problems

A road leading across the Bolivian Altiplano, with part of the Cordillera Real in the background

importance even though they are run at a loss. Without these services whole areas of Bolivia would be isolated—completely cut off from the rest of the country. In the 1970s new fleets of planes were purchased and many runways built, such as those of Trinidad in the north and Sucre in the south. A new airport and runway were also built at Tarija. In the past, without concrete runways, it was often impossible for days, and sometimes weeks, at a time to land during the rainy season. Flying can still be a big problem in Bolivia. Some of the old cargo planes are unable to fly higher than 3,660 metres (12,000 feet) and must, therefore, dodge the peaks of the Cordillera. On bad days, when visibility is poor, pilots can only navigate using a compass and stopwatch, though the fact that they have years of experience of flying though cloud and between the mountain peaks

81

makes air travel less hazardous than it sounds. LAB has a fine safety record. It is government policy to keep Bolivian internal flights operating even at a loss. Without them, many areas would suffer from the lack of any form of transport. Though air transport is very expensive, much freight is carried by air, such as the beef which is brought south from the cattle-raising areas of the Beni in the north-east. Even more surprising is the fact that passengers frequently carry livestock with them on their plane rides.

Water transport also has some importance in Bolivia. The route from Bolivia to Peru though Lake Titicaca links Bolivia with the Chilean Pacific port of Arica. A fleet of five steamers, made in Scotland, were carried piece by piece up to the Peruvian port of Puno on Lake Titicaca, then re-assembled. These steamers provide a service to Guagui on the Bolivian side

A steamer on the Bolivian side of Lake Titicaca

of the lake. Perhaps more important in the long run are the 8,850 kilometres (5,500 miles) of navigable river that exist in Bolivia. Most of the waters of the two northern rivers—the Mamore and the Beni—are already navigated into the River Madeira and on to the Amazon.

The iron industry being developed at Mutun, in the southeast, has generated interest by using the Paraguay River which flows into the Plate River in Argentina. Transport by other means in this remote part of the country would be too difficult and expensive. River transportation looks like being the answer to the problem.

There is no doubt that transport difficulties have held up, and continue to hold up, Bolivia's development. Bolivians feel, probably correctly, that if only the problems of transport could be solved then most of the country's other problems would be solved at the same time.

Culture

Dancing and music are an important part of Bolivian cultural life. At carnival times crocodiles of dancers will wind their way through the streets for days, as long as the music lasts and the *chicha*—a fermented maize drink—is flowing.

The music of Bolivia, and of the Andean mountains in general, is often described as sad but it can also be powerful and rhythmic. Certainly the music of the Andes can be haunting and beautiful when played on the instruments typical of the region. The *zamponas*—which are like Pan-pipes—are well known. Less well known are the *tarkas*—square, wooden flutes; the *bombo*—the bass drum that beats out the rhythms; the *quena*—a flute played throughout these mountains; and the *charanga*—made out of the spiny shell of an armadillo.

The love of folk music and dance is not confined to the country regions of Bolivia; the people of the towns value it just as highly. The Incas thought it necessary to get drunk at certain religious ceremonies. The Bolivian Indians have main-

An Aymara Indian playing the *zampona* (pan-pipes)

tained the custom! At celebrations vast quantities of *chicha*, or *pisco* (fermented grape juice) are drunk, and not only to wash down the *salteñas*—spicy meat pasties—which are always made for such occasions. Many dances were brought to Bolivia by the Spaniards, like the *cueca* which is similar to *flamenco*. Other dances have come from the Indians themselves, like the *huayños* from the Altiplano. *Bailecitos, taquivaris* and *carnavalitos* come from the valleys and tropical lowlands. All have both Spanish and Indian elements, like so many aspects of Bolivian life.

The chewing of *coca* leaves accompanies every part of Indian

Flute-makers selling their goods by the roadside in Cochabamba

life, including celebrations and festivities. *Coca* is believed to
have magical, even divine, properties and just as it enables Bolivians to work in extreme conditions, so it enables them to dance
non-stop for days. There is even a legend about its discovery.
Indians from the Altiplano travelled to the *yungas* looking for
fertile land. The valleys they discovered were fertile but
wooded, so they set fire to the vegetation to make a clearing.
The Storm God was angered by this and let loose a tempest
which put out the fire and destroyed all the green vegetation.
All, that is, except the *coca* bushes. The Indians, in their hunger,
ate the leaves and felt their strength returning. They have never

86

stopped eating *coca* and have woven their consumption of the plant into their religious and festive activities.

On feast days, like the Feast of the Virgin of Copacabana (a town near to Lake Titicaca), all the bright colourful clothes come out: brilliant red and green jackets for the men, with embroidered bell-bottomed trousers and bright new *chullos*—alpaca wool hats—worn on their heads. The women too will wear their best hats, and dresses (often of silk or velvet) puffed out with as many as twenty petticoats. Their blouses will be richly embroidered with silver an sequins.

Much Bolivian cultural and social life takes place in the open air. The carnivals are held out in the open, as are the dances

Aymara Indians at the Feast of the Virgin of Copacabana. On feast days, everyone dresses in bright colourful costumes

that accompany them. Along with the social life of the streets goes a great deal of gossip which is one of the main sources of information in Bolivia. Markets are places where people go to buy but also to talk and gossip with their neighbours. There is much entertainment at markets. No item is sold without haggling. Some people are practised and accomplished in the

A market on the Bolivian Altiplano—simple pots such as these have been made since Inca times

art and have followers in tow through the market just to listen to them.

There is much skill in evidence in Bolivian market places, from the woven clothes and blankets made by peasant women out of alpaca and llama wools to the simple pots made in the country. Working from basic materials, and using basic techniques, the Bolivians produce items of great beauty and usefulness, like those they have been producing since Inca times.

Bolivia's Future

There is a story, and it is probably only a story, that in the nineteenth century, President Melgarejo of Bolivia sent Queen Victoria's consul out of the capital in disgrace, without his clothes and sitting on a donkey. In her anger, Queen Victoria is said to have ordered a ship from the British navy to be positioned off the coast—only to be told Bolivia had no coast and that the British navy had no guns powerful enough to reach over the Andes. The Queen then, so it is said, had Bolivia removed from the map. The country no longer existed (as far as Britain was concerned). If such an event really did take place, it could go some way to explaining the lack of knowledge about Bolivia in Britain. However, it does not explain why other countries in Latin America are similarly unknown, not only in Britain, but also in other parts of the world.

Even Latin American countries know little about Bolivia, tucked as it is between much more powerful neighbours, almost in the middle of the Latin America continent. Yet its size and

90

the vastness of its resources mean that Bolivia is important. Its agricultural riches are sufficient not only for its own needs but also for those of Latin America and of other countries besides. The mineral wealth of Bolivia appears inexhaustible, requiring little more than better transportation to develop it for the benefit and use of others. But the country has been held back by its own political problems. A succession of presidents has inspired little confidence around the world and caused great disruption within Bolivia. There is need, too, for the education of Bolivia's Indian peoples so as to bring them fully into the life of the country. Nevertheless, this "little marvel" of which Bolivar spoke, with all its advantages, has great potential for future development and prosperity.

Index

93